ROYAL YACHTING ASSOCIATION

MOTOR CRUISING PRACTICAL COURSE NOTES

This booklet is aimed at illustrating and clarifying the PRACTICAL MOTOR CRUISING COURSES run by RYA recognised motor cruising schools. It should be used in conjunction with:

Day Skipper or Yachtmaster Shorebased Course Notes.
These booklets cover the theoretical side of navigation and support the *Day Skipper and Yachtmaster Shorebased courses* which are run by RYA recognised shorebased schools all over the country.

THE PRACTICAL COURSE

RYA recognised Motor Cruising schools run a series of courses from beginner to Yachtmaster. Details of the syllabi are included in the Motor Cruising Logbook G18 available from all schools and from the RYA.

Before attending a course you should ensure that it is the right one for you by checking the pre-course experience requirement. If you are uncertain about your level, discuss your experience with the school and let them advise you.

TAKING COMMAND

During the Day Skipper and Coastal Skipper courses you will be shown the pleasures and pitfalls of taking command. You will be taught how to take charge of the yacht for a short passage. This will involve planning the trip, briefing the crew, boat handling, navigation and many of the other skills described in these course notes. The instructor will encourage you to take responsibility for your decisions and illustrate that, in return for taking the credit when things go well, the skipper must also take responsibility when things go wrong. At the end of the course you should understand your strengths and weaknesses and have learnt how to undertake safe, relaxed passages as skipper in a limited area.

Your instructor will understand that you and the other course members are new to skippering and will make sure that the boat does not stand into danger. Finally remember that the reason for becoming mʳ ⸻⸻ᶠⁱᶜⁱᵉⁿᵗ is to gain more pleasure from the sport.

PARTS OF THE BOAT

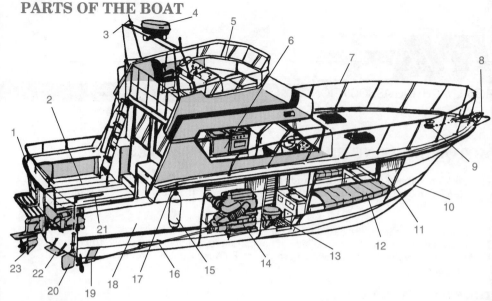

1. Transom
2. Cockpit
3. Radio aerial
4. Radar antenna
5. Flying bridge or fly bridge
6. Galley (kitchen) here part of deck house or saloon
7. Guardrail
8. Bow or stemhead roller   (for anchor line)
9. Windlass (anchor winch)
10. Chine (corner between topsides and bottom)
11. Forecabin or foc'sle
12. Bunk (bed)
13. Heads (toilet) (see page 4)
14. Engines (see pages 10-15)
15. Fenders
16. Stern gland bearing

17. Sidedecks
18. Topsides
19. 'P' bracket (holding prop shaft)
20. Rudder
21. 'Jury' or emergency tiller for steering
22. Trim tabs (see page 49)
23. Outdrive leg (see page 34)

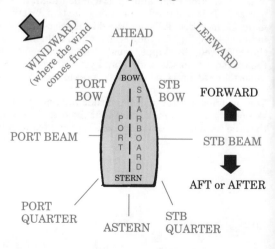

Use LEFT and RIGHT if it's clearer to *your* crew.

HULL SHAPES

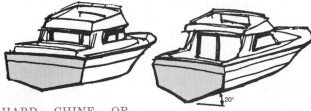

ROUND BILGE Usual for displacement or semi displacement craft that have to push through the water.

HARD CHINE OR SHALLOW VEE This shape will plane at high speed but 'slams' in waves.

DEEP VEE The deep 'veed' hull was developed to maintain high speed in waves.

HARBOUR TERMS harbours and coastlines abound with strangely named objects. This might help explain what the skipper is talking about

1. FAIRWAY Main channel into the harbour.
2. HEADLAND Prominent land sticking out.
3. HARBOUR ENTRANCE Often there are traffic laws to be obeyed.
4. BREAKWATER, GROYNE, TRAINING BANK Obstruction used to protect the land from the sea.
5. PILE MOORING Posts driven into the seabed to tie up to.
6. EBB When the tide is going out.
7. FLOOD OR FLOW When the tide is coming in.
8. CHANNEL Deep water route.
9. 'STEEP TO' CHANNEL EDGE Bottom gets deep quickly.
10. SHELVING Steep or gentle. How the bottom slopes.
11. SHOAL OR SHALLOWS
12. BEACON Navigation mark not always lit.

13. DOLPHIN Structure used as a navigation mark.
14. MOORING BUOYS When laid in a line called TROTS.
15. MARINA Enclosed area.
16. LOCK Used to keep the water level in the marina constant, while letting boats in and out.
17. CILL Sometimes instead of a 'lock' a cill or dam is used to keep enough water in the marina.
18. PONTOON Floating platform to moor boats to.
19. SLIPWAY Ramp to launch boats.
20. HARD Solid ground to launch small boats from.
21. CHANDLER Shop that sells boating equipment.
22. NAVIGATION BUOYS Buoys used to mark the edge of channels (see back cover).

3

THE HEADS

In the past sailors have used the front or 'head' of the boat for a lavatory and the name has stuck.

Basically they all suck in sea water through a seacock (valve) (A), flush the bowl and pump it out through another seacock (B) (or into a holding tank).

'Only things which have passed through the body' and moderate amounts of lavatory paper can be successfully flushed away.

So, women using sanitary towels should also take along a supply of disposal bags.

To prevent siphoning, the pipes carrying water to and from the lavatory rise above the water level and the seacocks are turned off at sea, when the system is not being used.

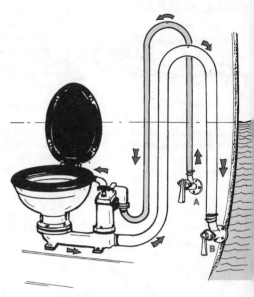

GAS

A strict sequence must be adhered to as bottled gas can be dangerous.

TO TURN ON

1. MAKE SURE ALL TAPS ARE CLOSED. ASK HOW THEY ALL WORK
2. TURN ON AT THE BOTTLE (A)
3. TURN ON THE MAIN COCK (B)
4. LIGHT THE MATCH
5. TURN ON THE BURNER
6. DISPOSE OF THE MATCH SAFELY

TO TURN OFF:-
If you are going to use the stove again soon:

1. TURN OFF THE MAIN COCK (B)
2. LET THE GAS BURN OUT
3. SHUT THE BURNER TAP

If you have finished with the stove

1. TURN OFF AT THE BOTTLE
2. LET THE GAS BURN OUT OF THE SYSTEM
3. SHUT OFF THE MAIN COCK
4. SHUT OFF THE BURNER TAP

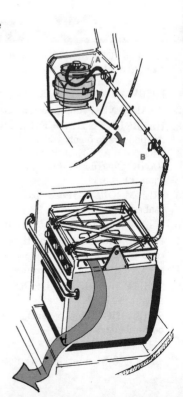

LIFE AFLOAT

A powerboat at sea is a lively beast, so the skipper should be aware of what other crew members are doing at all times. They can easily be thrown off balance and hurt themselves - or be lost overboard.

Slow down in choppy conditions, while meals are being prepared and warn people when the boat is going to make a violent movement (such as turning or crossing a wake).

Likewise *all* gear should be stowed securely and *not* 'just put down for a minute'. Large anchors can come adrift and be thrown through the wheelhouse and loose mooring lines can slide over the side and foul the props.

Even the humble wine bottle can take on a dangerous persona if it's sent flying across the cabin and loose packets of food can make an unwelcome addition to the decor.

Some countries have made the dangerous practice of 'bow riding' illegal and it's equally stupid to let people stand up near a working radar antenna.

CONTROLS

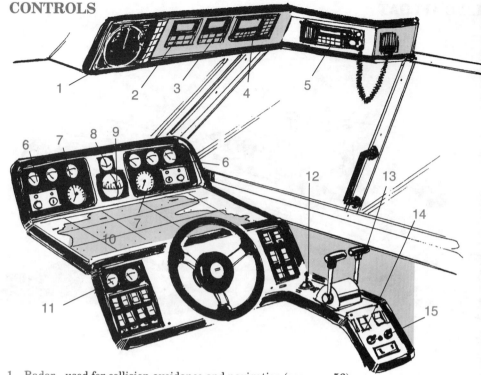

1. Radar - used for collision avoidance and navigation (see page 56).

2. Speed / Log - gives speed and distance.

3. Echo-sounder - shows depth of water (see page 59).

4. Decca / GPS - electronic position indicator (see page 58).

5. VHF Radio - for sending and receiving calls (see page 16).

6. Engine Instruments & Alarms - monitors *oil* pressure, *water* temperature and boost pressure.

7. Rev Counter - measures speed of engine.

8. Helm Indicator - shows position of the rudder.

9. Compass - points to magnetic north and shows course.

10. Chart / Pilot Notes holder - secure place for navigational charts.

11. Electrics - meters monitor electrical systems.

12. Bow-thruster - controls a small propeller in the bow to push the front sideways.

13. Throttles - control speed of engines.

14. Trim Tabs - set angle of trim (see page 49).

15. Power Trim - sets angle of outdrive leg (see page 48).

	**COMBINED GEAR & THROTTLE LEVERS** Here as you push the levers forward it engages the gear and opens the throttle on each engine. FOR: *Simple one handed use* AGAINST: *You could crash from ahead to astern without pausing and cause damage.*
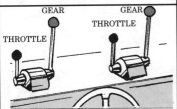	SEPARATE GEAR & THROTTLE LEVERS FOR EACH ENGINE FOR: *Throttles can be set to 'tick over' and manoeuvres carried out just using gears* AGAINST: *Confusing in an emergency - can't be used one-handed.*
	THROTTLES TOGETHER & GEARS TOGETHER FOR: *Throttles can be set at tick over and gears engaged with one hand* AGAINST: *Could be confused in an emergency*

All controls are different so make sure that you know what they all do before touching them. A great deal of damage can be caused by the wrong sequence of actions being carried out.

The general rule for gear and throttle controls is to move *slowly* and *gently - pausing* in neutral to give the engines time to slow down. NEVER SLAM THE ENGINES FROM AHEAD TO ASTERN.

Unfortunately the duplicate controls on the flybridge are not always wired up in the same way as those in the wheelhouse and alarms don't always work. *Always check.*

Trim controls are notoriously confusing (see page 49). Just touch the button for a second or two and *wait* to see what happens.

There is an ever increasing amount of gadgets adorning powerboats from electronic charts to bow-thrusters. Don't be a switch fiddler.....

...find out how to use the equipment.

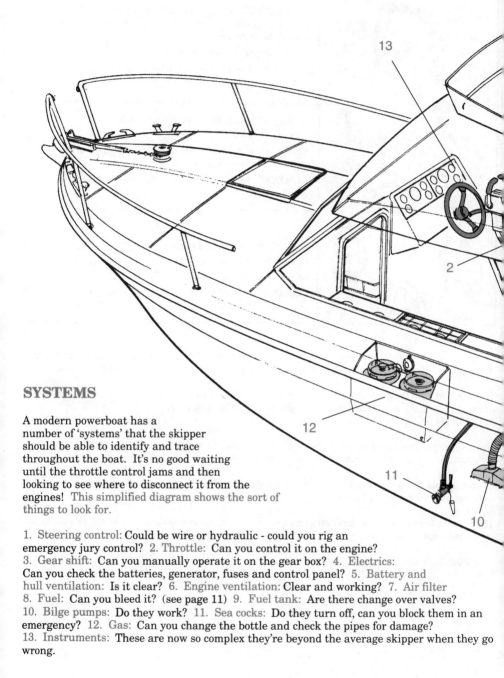

SYSTEMS

A modern powerboat has a
number of 'systems' that the skipper
should be able to identify and trace
throughout the boat. It's no good waiting
until the throttle control jams and then
looking to see where to disconnect it from the
engines! This simplified diagram shows the sort of
things to look for.

1. Steering control: Could be wire or hydraulic - could you rig an
emergency jury control? 2. Throttle: Can you control it on the engine?
3. Gear shift: Can you manually operate it on the gear box? 4. Electrics:
Can you check the batteries, generator, fuses and control panel? 5. Battery and
hull ventilation: Is it clear? 6. Engine ventilation: Clear and working? 7. Air filter
8. Fuel: Can you bleed it? (see page 11) 9. Fuel tank: Are there change over valves?
10. Bilge pumps: Do they work? 11. Sea cocks: Do they turn off, can you block them in an
emergency? 12. Gas: Can you change the bottle and check the pipes for damage?
13. Instruments: These are now so complex they're beyond the average skipper when they go
wrong.

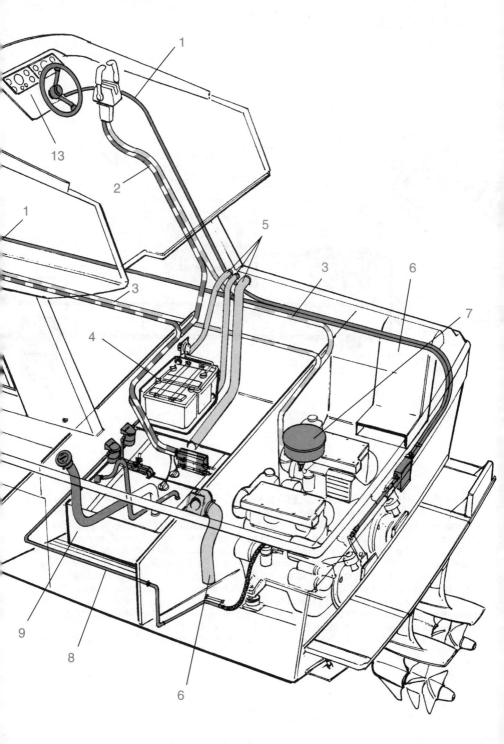

FUEL SYSTEM

ALL ENGINES ARE DIFFERENT - SO READ THE HANDBOOK. Spend some time in the engine compartment and trace the fuel system through so you know where *all* the *filters, cocks, returns and change over valves* are.

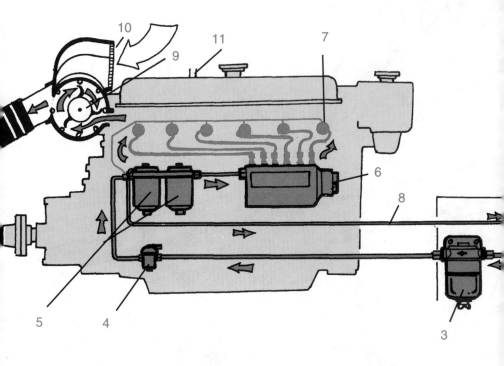

Marine diesels need CLEAN FUEL, FREE FROM *DIRT, WATER and AIR*. Any one of these will stop it dead! Someone on board should be able to change the filters and bleed the system. Fuel tanks can be anywhere in the boat and there might be several with various valves and cocks connecting them. Try to keep them full to prevent moisture condensing in the air above the fuel. Shut off cocks and drain plugs isolate the tank for cleaning. Water separators and primary filters extract most of the dirt and moisture from the fuel, while the fuel pump drives the fuel through an even finer secondary filter. The injection pump measures out the fuel and delivers it, at a very high pressure, to the cylinders via the injectors. Excess fuel returns to the tank via the fuel leak-off return pipe. Diesels run on a mixture of fuel and air which explodes when it is compressed in the cylinders. High powered engines use an enormous amount of air which is sucked in by a turbo-charger. This is like a large fan which is driven by the exhaust gases leaving the engine. The air is kept clean with an air filter.

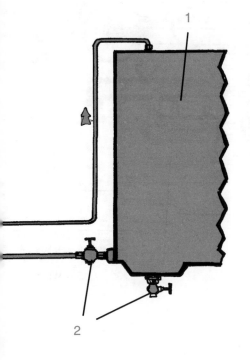

1. Fuel tanks

2. Shut-off cock and stripping valve (tank drain)

3. Water separator / primary filter

4. Fuel feed or lift pump

5. Secondary filters (one or two)

6. Injection pump

7. Injectors

8. Fuel leak-off return pipe

9. Turbo-charger

10. Air filter

11. Engine breather

The simplest and best fuel system is to have a separate tank and supply for each engine. So if one stops due to loss of fuel or air, water or dirt in the system, the other engine won't stop simultaneously.

Total loss of power could be embarrassing or dangerous depending on the circumstances.

In heavy weather sediment in the tanks could be drawn into the system or air introduced if the fuel level is low and the angle of heel excessive. If this happens the filters will need changing, the tanks topping up and the system bled of air.

Bleeding. The handbook will explain the procedure for your engine but in principle you always start at the tank and end at the injectors. However some modern diesels will bleed themselves

COOLING AND LUBRICATION

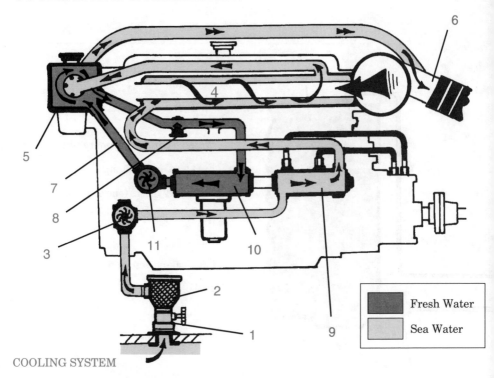

	Fresh Water
	Sea Water

COOLING SYSTEM

1. Sea cock lets sea water into the cooling system.

2. Strainer filters out any debris.

3. Sea water pump drives the water around.

4. Inter-cooler cools the hot compressed air from the turbo-charger.

5. Heat exchanger lets the sea water cool the closed fresh water cooling system.

6. Wet exhaust takes the salt water out with the exhaust gases.

7. Fresh water system circulates fresh water around the engine for cooling.

8. Thermostat opens when the engine reaches a set temperature.

9. Gear box cooler cools the oil in the gearbox.

10. Engine oil cooler.

11. Fresh water pump.

LUBRICATION

Oil levels for the engine and gearbox are usually checked with dipsticks. The oil system is cooled with the warmer fresh water to help in cold conditions, while the cold sea water is used first to cool the very hot turbo charged air and then used to cool the fresh water.

PRE-START CHECKS (See your handbook)

OIL LEVELS

Check lubricant levels in both engine and gearbox. *(Some gearboxes are checked when engine is running)*

Remember, levels can vary between a hot and cold engine.

WATER

Check coolant level in heat exchanger header tank.

FUEL

Check fuel levels.

COCKS & SWITCHES

• Check all fuel and water cocks are open and all switches are in their starting positions.

STARTING

• You may need some throttle *(about half is normal)* to start the engines.

• Don't use a series of small stabs at the starter button - press firmly for 20 seconds.

• If the engines don't start let the starter motors cool down before trying again.

• When the engines fire, reduce the engine revs to a smooth idle (say 1000 rpm).

• Check all gauges are normal.

• Check cooling water is discharging - normally out of the exhaust pipe.

• Diesel engines are best warmed up under load - so get underway when all the checks have been completed.

• Increase speed gradually to allow the engines to warm up - it's best to avoid maximum revs. for the first 10 minutes.

KEEP A GOOD MACHINERY LOG WITH ALL THE *NORMAL TEMPERATURES AND PRESSURES* FOR THE ENGINE NOTED.

Things that change slowly during the season can go unnoticed *but* by logging all the details at regular intervals a pattern might evolve which will help the engineer's diagnosis, before real trouble develops.

SIMPLE ENGINE FAULTS

BLOCKED FUEL FILTERS - MOST COMMON.

SYMPTOMS
The first sign may be loss of power at full speed.
Why? The filter cannot pass the amount of fuel demanded by the engine at maximum load.

DIAGNOSIS
When the throttle is closed slightly (reducing the amount of fuel demanded) the engine revs steady up.

This point will slowly decrease (as the filter becomes more blocked) until only idle speed is possible and the engine will soon stop.

REMEDY
Change the fuel filters and re-start the engine.

With twin engines be aware that the second engine may soon develop the same fault, so it might be useful to change its fuel filter at the same time. (Note dirty fuel can take a while to pass through the system so several filter changes may be necessary.)

BLOCKED SALT WATER INLET FILTERS - COMMON

SYMPTOMS
Total blockage will cause the engine to overheat very quickly - but careful observation will often detect a partial blockage before this occurs.

The salt water system pumps more water than the engine needs to cool it - in fact the water is still quite cool when it leaves the engine to cool the exhaust system.

DIAGNOSIS
An increase in steam at the exhaust discharge is the first sign of overheating - compare both exhausts to see which is faulty.

REMEDY
Check the salt water filters either through the 'clear' lids or by stopping the engines and looking inside for a blockage. If they are OK it could be the sea water pump is faulty or there is a leak in the sea-water system either discharging into the engine or into the bilge.

With the large amounts of water that are being pumped, a bilge alarm or automatic pump (with an indicator light by the helm) is a good safeguard against filling the boat up!

BLOCKED AIR FILTERS - UNUSUAL

SYMPTOMS
Air filter blockage is sometimes caused by some other engine room incident - such as a belt slipping and giving off a lot of dust.
The first sign is a loss of power at full load.

Why? The correct amount of air can't pass through the filter at full throttle. The engine starts *'hunting'* (revs falling and rising) at full load and black smoke will appear at the exhaust as the fuel isn't being burnt correctly.

DIAGNOSIS
Ease back throttles – *'hunting'* stops.

REMEDY
Clean filters or remove in an emergency.

Minimum spares to carry for short cruises

Fuel Enough for passage plus 20% - preferably in isolated tanks, so you don't lose the lot if one leaks. *Remember range can be increased by slowing down.*
Fuel filters 2 changes, primary and secondary.
Lub oil Capacity for 1 engine plus top-up. If the gear box, generator, steering gear, trim tabs etc. use different oils the same rule applies.
Pump impellors 1 per pump, plus various lengths of hoses, special bends and clips.
Liquid sealant for water systems Often a leak can be temporarily repaired with a special sealant mixed in with water.
Vee belts One complete set plus some link belting for quick repairs at sea. Link belts can be made up to any length and tensioned easily. Even if the alternator seizes, a belt can be made up to drive the water pump provided the path is clear across the engine. (Best to check this in harbour).

Remember, a simple fault such as a slipping belt can cause the engine to overheat (fresh water pump) and the electrical charging rate to fall (alternator)...

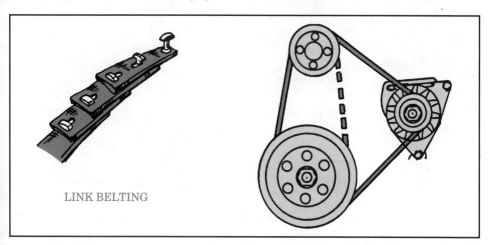

LINK BELTING

..SO, READ THE HANDBOOK, GET FAMILIAR WITH YOUR ENGINE AND CARRY AN ADEQUATE TOOLKIT

VHF RADIO DISTRESS CALL

A distress call is sent when there is *GRAVE AND IMMINENT DANGER* to a vessel or a person and *IMMEDIATE ASSISTANCE* is required.

HOW TO SEND A DISTRESS CALL

Switch on power, switch on radio, select *CH16*, turn to high power. Push press-to-transmit switch and speak slowly and distinctly.

- MAYDAY, MAYDAY, MAYDAY.
- This is (Yacht's Name 3 times)
- MAYDAY (Yacht's Name)
- Position (see below)
- Nature of distress
- Any extra information which might help
- Over
- Take your finger off the transmit button

Turning on the set etc. can be forgotten in an emergency so make up a reminder card and stick it up near the radio.

MAYDAY is the international distress signal.

The 'name' and the word 'yacht' helps the searchers know what they are looking for.

'I require immediate assistance' and include number of people on board, whether you are going to abandon ship or have fired flares etc.

'Over' means please reply.

AN URGENCY CALL

An urgency call is used when you have a *VERY IMPORTANT MESSAGE* to send covering *SAFETY*.

PAN PAN, PAN PAN, PAN PAN,
All stations (3 times)
This is (Yacht's Name 3 times)

- Position
- Nature of urgency
- Assistance required
- Over

The advantage of an urgency call is that it lets the world know that you are in some sort of trouble without launching all the rescue services at that moment.

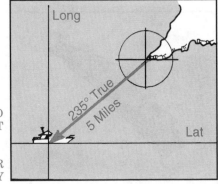

PREFIX A CALL TO A BRITISH COASTAL RADIO STATION WITH *PAN PAN MEDICO,* TO GET MEDICAL ADVICE.

KEEP TRANSMITTING AT REGULAR INTERVALS EVEN IF YOU DON'T GET A REPLY SO THE RESCUERS CAN HOME IN ON YOU.

EPIRB Emergency Position Indicating Radio Beacons will raise the alarm and help the rescue services to find you.
Positions must be given in Lat or Long or TRUE bearings FROM a charted position with distance off. (eg, Position 235° from South Head, 5 miles.)
If it's a DECCA position, say so as any errors can be duplicated in the rescue craft's set.

DISTRESS SIGNALS can be sent by waving your arms, continuous fog horn blast, SOS by any means, NC by flags or a ball over a square shape or flares and rockets.

HAND HELD PIN-POINT
FLARES & SMOKE   Visible 3 - 7 miles

PARACHUTE ROCKET Visible 28 miles

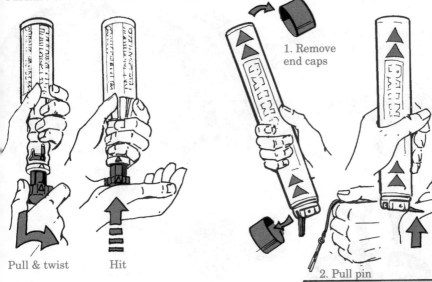

1. Remove end caps

Pull & twist   Hit

3. Press trigger

2. Pull pin

PARACHUTE ROCKETS
(1) These need to be fired slightly DOWNWIND as the rocket always curves towards the wind.
(2) In low cloud fire 45° DOWNWIND so flare deploys below 1000 ft.

USE PINPOINT FLARES TO GUIDE RESCUE CRAFT

wind

45°

FIRE
Fire needs: Heat, Fuel and Oxygen - cut out any one, and the fire goes out.

ALWAYS USE AN EXTINGUISHER UPRIGHT
- Never open engine box fully (as this will feed air to the fire) just open it a crack and use extinguisher.

- NEVER BREATHE IN THE SMOKE it could contain burning plastic which is poisonous.

FIRE BLANKETS CAN SMOTHER A SMALL FIRE. Hold like this to protect your hands.

- If a person's on fire push them over (so flames rise away from the face) and smother flames away from face.

17

SAFETY GEAR

Lifejackets

Each crew member must know how to use a lifejacket. Basically they go over the head and are tied or buckled at the side.

Adopt this position in water to keep spray from nose and preserve body heat.

LIFTING HANDLE

WHISTLE

REFLECTIVE TAPE

INFLATION TUBE

Safety harness

HOOK ON WHEN:
- The skipper tells you
- In rough weather - especially if you're on the flybridge or foredeck
- At night

There are various types of hooks but make sure yours works and is clipped onto something strong. Always clip on so you can't be thrown over the side.

Liferafts

UNLESS THE BOAT IS SINKING FAST, OR ON FIRE, DON'T USE THE LIFERAFT. You will stand more chance of being rescued, and suffer less from exposure in a flooded boat, than in a tiny liferaft.

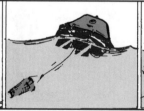

The static line, once attached to the boat, might have to be pulled 25ft or more before inflation. Put a strong man in first for stability and to help weaker members aboard.

Cut the static line, stream the drogue to stop drift and add stability. Unplug the light during the day to save battery power.

Close main canopy, take seasick tablets, post a look-out, inflate double floor, tie in pump, spread out weight in rough weather or huddle together to keep warm.

RESCUE

- Lifeboats and some helicopters can home in on your VHF or EPIRB - so keep calling at intervals.
- Get crew ready to abandon ship in case things get worse.
- Wear lifejackets and warm clothing and take only *small* valuables.
- If you can see the rescue craft tell them your position: 'We're 20° to the right of you 1/2 mile etc.'
- They might ask you to use a pin-point flare.

LIFEBOAT

- The lifeboat *might* take you in tow. *If you can,* prepare the boat by rigging a line around several strong points (or right round the deckhouse) if you're unsure of the strength of your cleats.

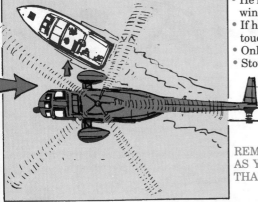

Warn them if your props are fouled

- The cox'n might pass you a line so you'll need to be clipped on and wearing a lifejacket. Only have 1 or 2 crew on the foredeck.
- They might put a man on board to organise everything or throw you a *heaving line* - use this to pull in the *tow rope.*
- If they can't get close, they might fire a thin *gun-line* – use this to haul in the *heaving line* THEN pull in the *towline.*
- Secure the tow line.

AT NIGHT
You'll need to show your position with a flare or a searchlight. Shine this *straight up* for a *lifeboat* BUT *straight ahead* for a helicopter.

HELICOPTER
- Brief your crew early - it'll be too noisy later.
- He'll probably ask you to head into the wind.

BUT EVERY RESCUE IS DIFFERENT SO DO EXACTLY AS YOU'RE TOLD.

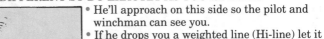

- He'll approach on this side so the pilot and winchman can see you.
- If he drops you a weighted line (Hi-line) let it touch the water first (to earth it).
- Only pull in when directed.
- Stow end in bucket so it doesn't foul up.

NEVER TIE IT ON.

- He may lower the winchman directly on to the deck

REMEMBER - THEY'RE THE EXPERTS - DO AS YOU'RE TOLD AND DON'T FORGET TO THANK THEM!

19

ROPE WORK

BOWLINE is the best knot for forming an eye or loop. It doesn't jam and can be undone easily. There are several ways of tying it but this *twisting* method is the simplest.

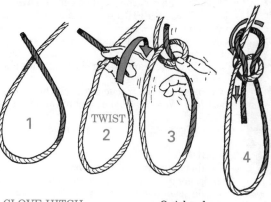

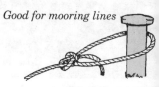

Good for mooring lines

CLOVE HITCH

Quick release loop

Used for temporarily attaching fenders as it can be adjusted easily or to form a sliding noose.

ROUND TURN & TWO HALF HITCHES

Hitches should go the same way

Ideal for mooring lines as it can be let go under tension. Also makes a stronger fender attachment.

CLEATS
Secure by taking a turn around the *back* of the cleat then add *figure of eights* for friction.

Twisted locking turn

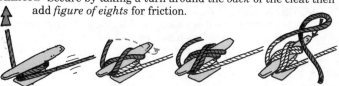

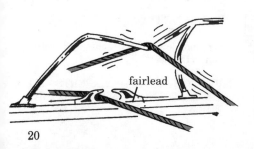

fairlead

Cleats come in all shapes and sizes but basically the more turns you add the more grip it has.

Always take lines under the rail and through a fairlead or this will happen when any load comes on the line.

COILS

A regular rhythm of say an arm's width creates an even coil.

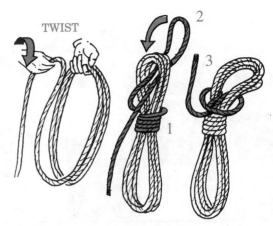

TWIST

Laid rope needs to be coiled *clockwise* and given a *right hand twist* in each turn. Plaited rope tends to form 'figure of eights'. Both can be stored like this.

THROWING A LINE

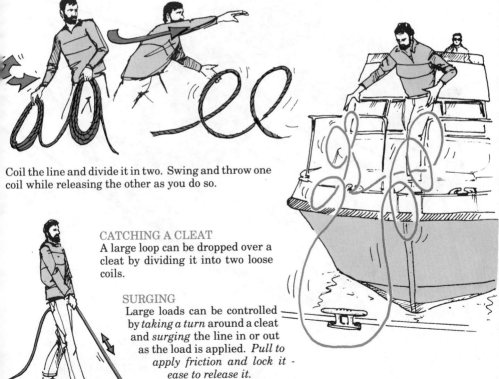

Coil the line and divide it in two. Swing and throw one coil while releasing the other as you do so.

CATCHING A CLEAT
A large loop can be dropped over a cleat by dividing it into two loose coils.

SURGING
Large loads can be controlled by *taking a turn* around a cleat and *surging* the line in or out as the load is applied. *Pull to apply friction and lock it - ease to release it.*

MOORING ALONGSIDE

USE A
FENDER
✔

DON'T FEND OFF BY
PUTTING PARTS OF
YOUR BODY BETWEEN
TWO BOATS

DON'T EVER JUMP FOR IT

Ask permission to be alongside another boat.
Tight springs and breastropes are important to
hold the raft together.
Rig adequate fenders.

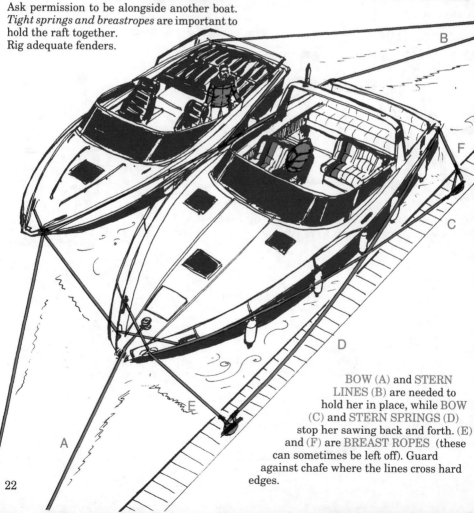

BOW (A) and STERN
LINES (B) are needed to
hold her in place, while BOW
(C) and STERN SPRINGS (D)
stop her sawing back and forth. (E)
and (F) are BREAST ROPES (these
can sometimes be left off). Guard
against chafe where the lines cross hard
edges.

MAKING FAST ALONGSIDE

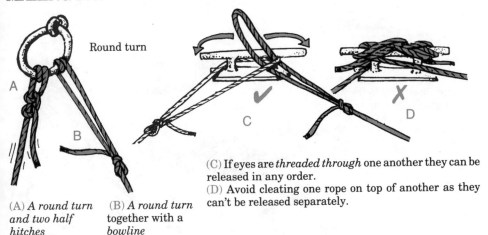

Round turn

(A) *A round turn and two half hitches*

(B) *A round turn together with a bowline*

(C) If eyes are *threaded through* one another they can be released in any order.

(D) Avoid cleating one rope on top of another as they can't be released separately.

ALLOWING FOR THE TIDAL RISE AND FALL

All mooring lines should be at least 3 times as long as the *rise* or *fall* of the tide. Nylon is good as it will stretch but must be protected from chafe. It makes sense to leave someone to adjust lines and fenders as things can catch up at awkward moments.

FENDER CARE

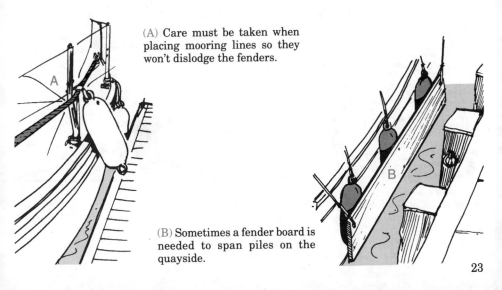

(A) Care must be taken when placing mooring lines so they won't dislodge the fenders.

(B) Sometimes a fender board is needed to span piles on the quayside.

23

USING LINES

Always let the
short end slip.

Never let lines trail in the water as
they might foul the propeller.

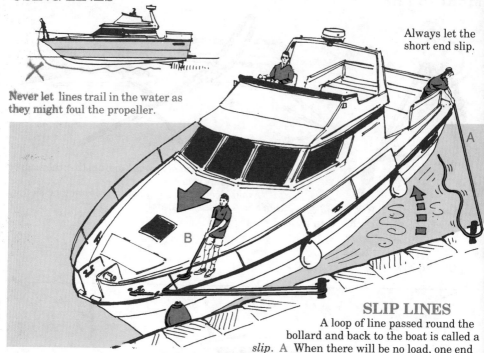

SLIP LINES

A loop of line passed round the
bollard and back to the boat is called a
slip. A When there will be no load, one end
can be held by the crew above the rail until it needs
to be released. B But if the skipper is going to power against it to turn the boat, the line must
come back through a fairlead and a turn must be taken around a cleat.

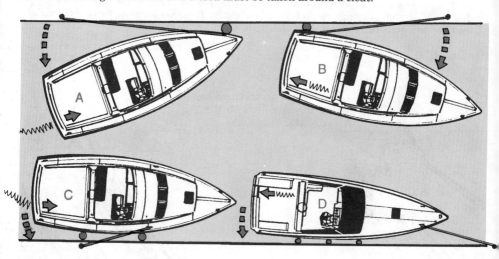

Powering against a line can push the boat away from the wall A and B or bring it into the wall
and hold it there. C and D.

Let the cleat take the weight - not the crew! (See page 42 for leaving without springs.)

LEAVING ALONGSIDE

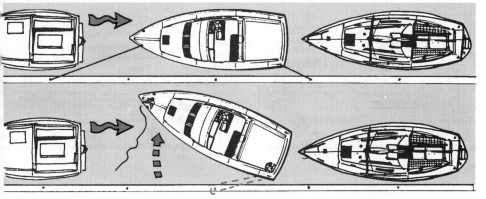

Be aware of what the tide or wind will do when you let go the line. Here a short stern spring (dotted) has been rigged to stop the boat crashing backwards while the tide pushes the bow out.

LEAVING A RAFT
A Here the tidal stream will tear the raft apart.

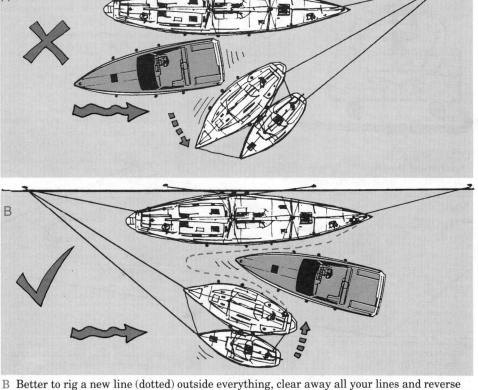

B Better to rig a new line (dotted) outside everything, clear away all your lines and reverse out leaving the current to close the boats together again. Fend off as you leave.

TIDAL STREAMS

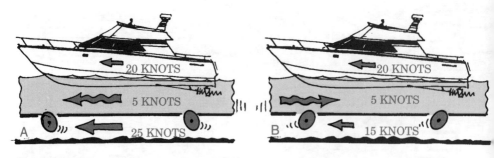

The tidal stream can either speed you up (A) or slow you down (B).

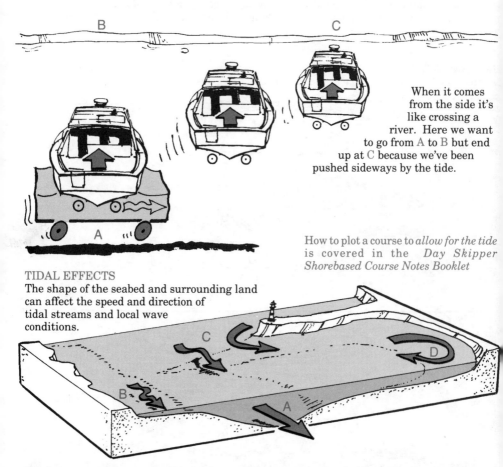

When it comes from the side it's like crossing a river. Here we want to go from A to B but end up at C because we've been pushed sideways by the tide.

How to plot a course to *allow for the tide* is covered in the *Day Skipper Shorebased Course Notes Booklet*

TIDAL EFFECTS
The shape of the seabed and surrounding land can affect the speed and direction of tidal streams and local wave conditions.

Tidal streams in deep water (A) are stronger than those in the shallows (B). Headlands and 'ledges' (C) can increase the rate of flow and cause 'overfalls' as the water rushes through the narrowed gap. Bays can cause back eddies (D) where the tidal stream turns back on itself.

WIND EFFECT

Most powerboats tend to get the bows blown off downwind. In fact some will be blown faster sideways than fore and aft. This all has to be allowed for when manoeuvring. But all boats are different so experiment and see what happens - it can be quite dramatic on a windy day!

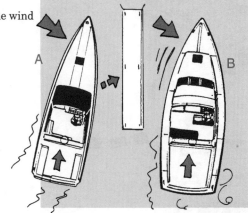

LEAVING
Here, boat (A) is finding it hard to leave the pontoon as a strong wind is pinning it in.

Boat (B), on the other hand, has the wind helping it by letting it gently blow off the pontoon. (See page 42)

ARRIVING
Boat (A) is letting the wind blow it in.

Boat (B) keeps having its bows blown off the pontoon (See page 42)

PICKING UP A MOORING BUOY.
Many modern powerboats (A) find it easier to hold their sterns to the wind controlling their position with their engines.

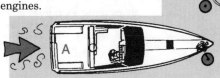

Boat (B)'s bows keep blowing away from the buoy as she slows down.

27

PROPELLER EFFECT

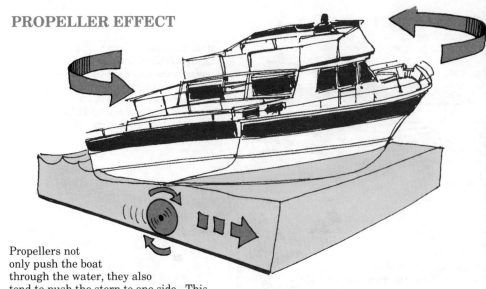

Propellers not
only push the boat
through the water, they also
tend to push the stern to one side. This
is known as 'Prop effect' or 'Paddle Wheel effect'. Here we have a left-handed prop pushing the
stern to starboard when motoring astern. A right handed prop has the opposite effect.

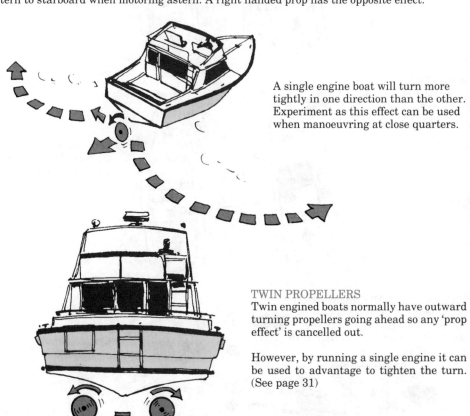

A single engine boat will turn more
tightly in one direction than the other.
Experiment as this effect can be used
when manoeuvring at close quarters.

TWIN PROPELLERS
Twin engined boats normally have outward
turning propellers going ahead so any 'prop
effect' is cancelled out.

However, by running a single engine it can
be used to advantage to tighten the turn.
(See page 31)

USING TWIN PROPELLERS
Offset effect

As the propellers are offset from the centre line of the boat, by running just one we can actually turn the boat without using the rudders.

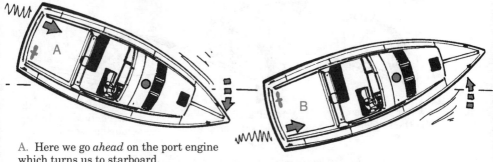

A. Here we go *ahead* on the port engine which turns us to starboard.

B. Here we just use the starboard engine in *ahead* to go to port. The opposite occurs in reverse.

Try it out using this book as the boat!

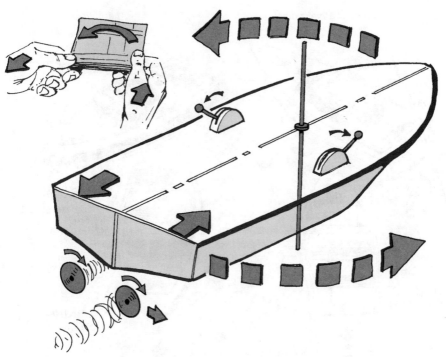

For a really tight turn run one engine in *ahead* and the other in *astern*.

Here we are running the starboard engine *ahead*..
..its *prop effect* and *offset effect* are pushing the stern to starboard. Also we are running the port engine in *reverse*...
..its *prop effect* and *offset effect* are also pushing the stern to starboard.
The combined effect will turn the boat in her own length...
..see page 33 on how to control it.

RUDDER EFFECT

Stern moves this way

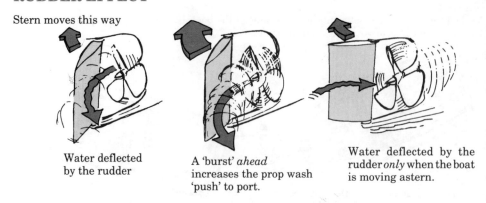

Water deflected
by the rudder

A 'burst' *ahead*
increases the prop wash
'push' to port.

Water deflected by the
rudder *only* when the boat
is moving astern.

Rudders steer the boat by deflecting water thrown back by the propeller or the water displaced by the boat moving forward. The effect can be increased with a 'burst' ahead but won't work in reverse as the prop wash goes forward. Therefore steering in reverse in a single engined boat is less positive.

TURNING

Pivot point

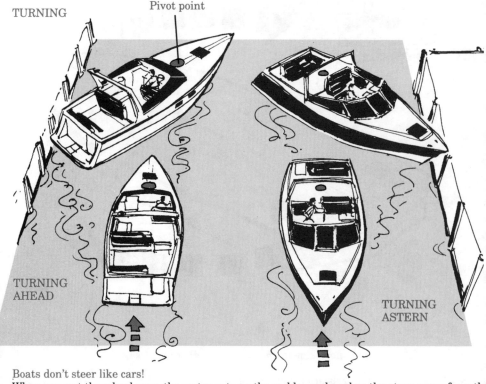

TURNING
AHEAD

TURNING
ASTERN

Boats don't steer like cars!
When you put the wheel over, the water acts on the rudder and pushes the stern away from the direction you want to go.
In *ahead* the boat pivots *about 1/3 from the bow*.
In *astern* the boat pivots *about 1/3 from the stern*.
Here we misjudged it and will hit the wall in both cases.

30

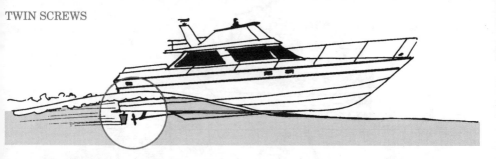

On high speed craft the rudders are quite small and less effective at low speeds. Twin propellers or screws mean you won't need bursts of power to increase the prop wash effect on the rudders. Their prop and offset effects are more powerful. BUT don't forget to use the rudders as well as it will tighten your turning circle. (See 2 below).

How tight do you want to turn?

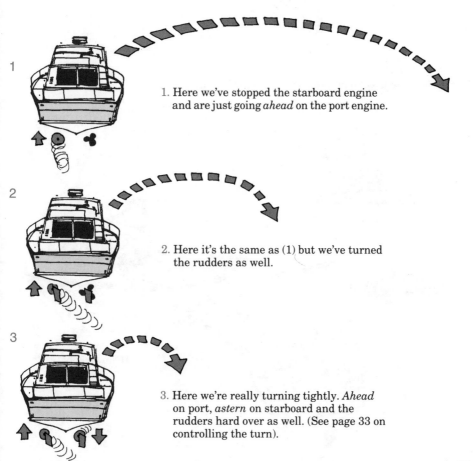

1. Here we've stopped the starboard engine and are just going *ahead* on the port engine.

2. Here it's the same as (1) but we've turned the rudders as well.

3. Here we're really turning tightly. *Ahead* on port, *astern* on starboard and the rudders hard over as well. (See page 33 on controlling the turn).

TURNING
Single screw

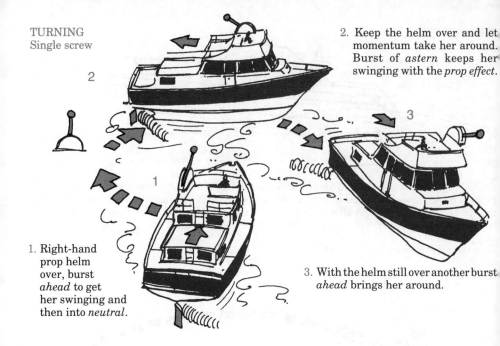

2. Keep the helm over and let momentum take her around. Burst of *astern* keeps her swinging with the *prop effect*.

1. Right-hand prop helm over, burst *ahead* to get her swinging and then into *neutral*.

3. With the helm still over another burst *ahead* brings her around.

LET THE WIND HELP
If there is a strong wind blowing use it to help blow the bow around.

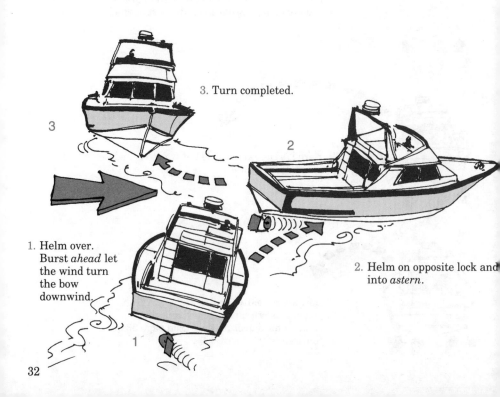

3. Turn completed.

1. Helm over. Burst *ahead* let the wind turn the bow downwind.

2. Helm on opposite lock and into *astern*.

TURNING ON THE SPOT

By balancing the throttles and running the engines in opposite directions a twin-screwed boat can be made to turn on the spot.

Pivot

Ahead

Astern

With the engines on tick-over balance the throttles so she doesn't go *ahead* or *astern*.

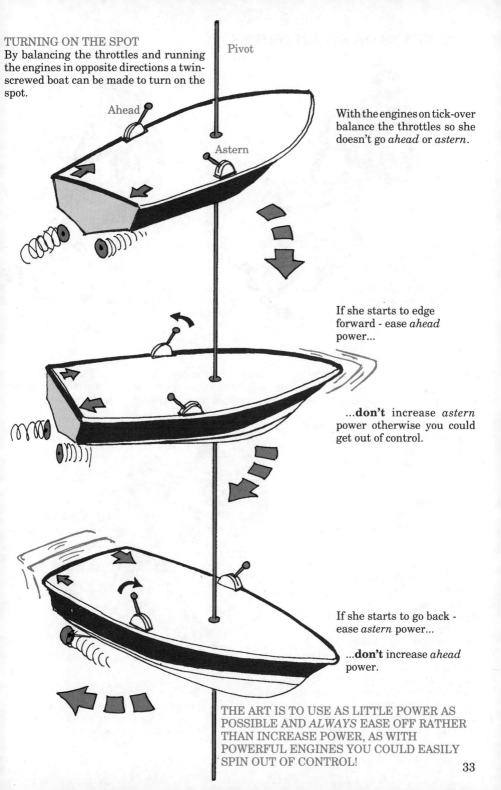

If she starts to edge forward - ease *ahead* power...

...**don't** increase *astern* power otherwise you could get out of control.

If she starts to go back - ease *astern* power...

...**don't** increase *ahead* power.

THE ART IS TO USE AS LITTLE POWER AS POSSIBLE AND *ALWAYS* EASE OFF RATHER THAN INCREASE POWER, AS WITH POWERFUL ENGINES YOU COULD EASILY SPIN OUT OF CONTROL!

33

OUTDRIVES OR STERN DRIVES

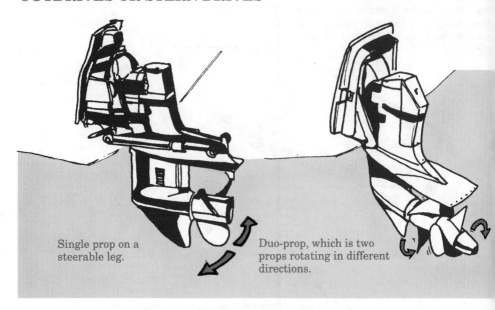

Single prop on a steerable leg.

Duo-prop, which is two props rotating in different directions.

An outdrive doesn't have a rudder so can only steer when there is power on, and the propeller is driving. However, as the drive can be angled away from the centre-line of the boat, sharper turns can be achieved in close-quarters manoeuvring than with a conventional rudder system.

There are two basic types - a single screw and a contra rotating duo-prop. Both claim different advantages. Any *prop effect* can be eliminated on the single screw by steering slightly to one side while on the duo-prop it's naturally cancelled out.

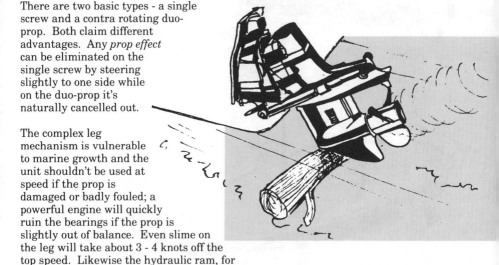

The complex leg mechanism is vulnerable to marine growth and the unit shouldn't be used at speed if the prop is damaged or badly fouled; a powerful engine will quickly ruin the bearings if the prop is slightly out of balance. Even slime on the leg will take about 3 - 4 knots off the top speed. Likewise the hydraulic ram, for raising and lowering the leg, should always be left so the ram is inside the cylinder and therefore protected from fouling, which would eventually damage the rubber seals.

The leg will 'knock-up' to protect the prop and the angle of the leg can be adjusted for running in shallow water or boat trim (see page 48).

STEERING WITH TWIN OUTDRIVES

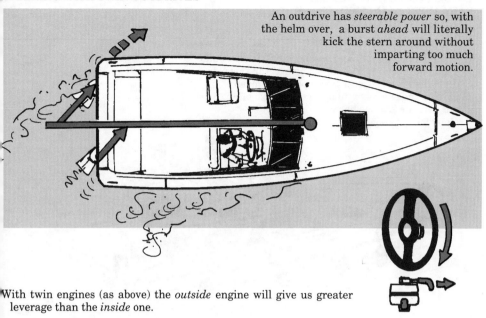

An outdrive has *steerable power* so, with the helm over, a burst *ahead* will literally kick the stern around without imparting too much forward motion.

With twin engines (as above) the *outside* engine will give us greater leverage than the *inside* one.

So the general rules for most tight manoeuvres are:

- STOP THE BOAT / STEER THE LEG / APPLY THE POWER
  simplified as:- STOP, STEER, POWER

- To turn RIGHT it's RIGHT WHEEL and power on LEFT ENGINE
  or to turn LEFT it's LEFT WHEEL and power on RIGHT ENGINE
  simplified as:- RIGHT WHEEL / LEFT ENGINE
                      LEFT WHEEL / RIGHT ENGINE

These rules work for both *AHEAD* and *ASTERN* with only a few exceptions (see page 42).

OFFSET EFFECT

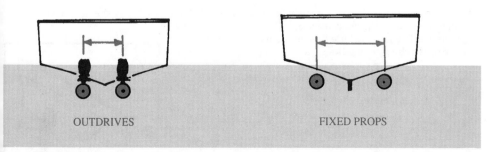

OUTDRIVES   FIXED PROPS

The *offset effect* (powering one engine against another) to turn the boat in its own length is usually less with outdrives as they're usually set closer together than fixed props.

COMING ALONGSIDE
EASY APPROACH - TWIN PROPS

1. If there is plenty of room and no wind you can make
   a long approach at a shallow angle at the slowest
   controllable speed which will probably mean
   putting the engines into neutral every so often to
   see how she 'carries her way' or glides
   along with no power.

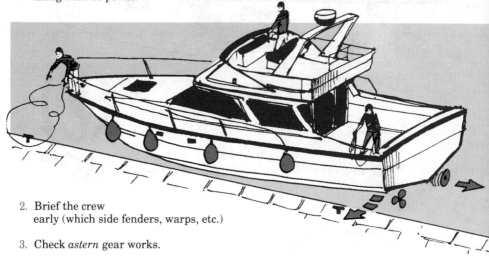

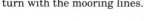

2. Brief the crew
   early (which side fenders, warps, etc.)

3. Check *astern* gear works.

4. Make a dummy run to see how the tide affects your boat. Look for 'back
   eddies' or 'flukey' winds alongside the dock. Look for clues like tight
   mooring lines or flags.

5. If 'tick-over' with both engines is too fast just put the *outside* engine in gear
   and use that for the approach.

6. Try to line up something ashore to see if you're drifting sideways.

7. Ask permission if you are going to lie alongside another vessel.

8. Check again that the crew know what is required of them. it is up to the helmsman to
   stop the boat in the right position. Don't expect the crew
   to fend off or jump ashore to stop the boat by taking a
   turn with the mooring lines.

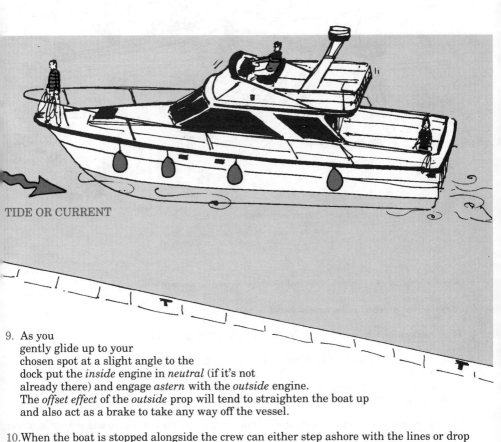

TIDE OR CURRENT

9. As you
   gently glide up to your
   chosen spot at a slight angle to the
   dock put the *inside* engine in *neutral* (if it's not
   already there) and engage *astern* with the *outside* engine.
   The *offset effect* of the *outside* prop will tend to straighten the boat up
   and also act as a brake to take any way off the vessel.

10. When the boat is stopped alongside the crew can either step ashore with the lines or drop
    a loop over a dock bollard or cleat.

STERN DRIVE APPROACH

1. The initial approach angle is just the same as with twin props.

2. With lightweight high powered craft which are easily affected by cross winds, it might be
   necessary to keep a little more way on the boat just as you come alongside the berth. Put
   the engines into *neutral*, steer the props towards the dock and engage *astern* an the
   outside engine.

AS ALWAYS WITH ANY MANOEUVRE - DO IT AS SLOWLY AS POSSIBLE, WITH AS
LITTLE THROTTLE AS POSSIBLE.

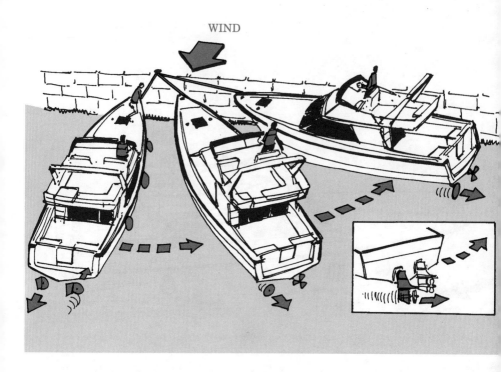

WIND

1. Have a line secured to the bow and fenders rigged down one side.

2. Approach at a good angle almost *'head to wind'*.

3. Hold her against the wind while the bowman secures the line.

4. Now you are safe you can just blow back on the bow line.

5. To get her to swing in alongside, go astern on the *outside engine* - it might need a touch of *ahead* on the inside engine to get her started.

6. Stop the *inside* prop and also stop the *outside* prop from time to time, so she swings in under her own momentum.

7. If she's swinging too fast stop the prop or go *astern* on the *inside* prop or *ahead* on the *outside* prop.

8. With stern drives the power can be angled, so turn the legs and let the outside prop pull you in. Again stop the prop or go *ahead* to control the swing.

ONSHORE WIND APPROACH - Twin props

1. Have all lines and fenders ready.
2. Approach gently and stop opposite your chosen spot: in strong winds you'll have to stop further out.
3. Turn the helm to windward and go *ahead* on *inside* prop to counteract the bow blowing downwind or go astern on the outside prop and turn the helm to leeward if you are ahead of the berth.

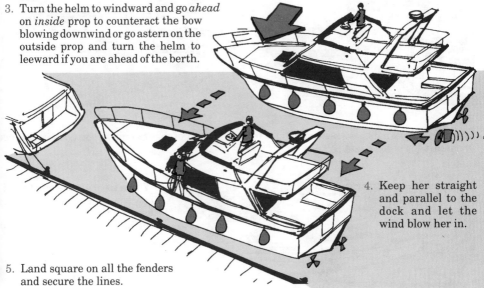

4. Keep her straight and parallel to the dock and let the wind blow her in.

5. Land square on all the fenders and secure the lines.

ONSHORE APPROACH - Stern drives

1. The approach is the same as with twin props but if it's a lightweight craft you'll need to turn her up into the wind at quite an angle, as the bow will start to blow sideways very quickly.

WIND

2. Control angle of approach with *inside* prop to keep her parallel.

3. Land square on all the fenders as it has been known for a fender to burst if it takes the full weight of the boat.

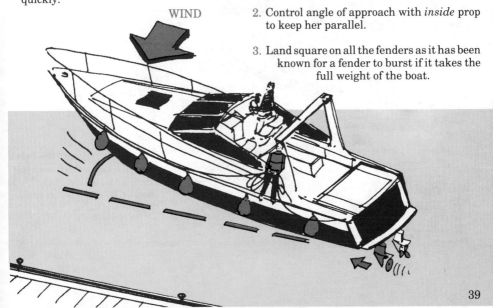

MARINAS

WIND

In strong cross winds always keep to the windward side A of the channel so you don't get pinne
in against the other boats B.

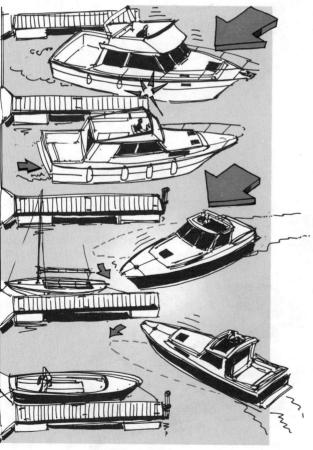

With a strong cross wind the bow can blow off before you have a chance to leave the berth.

To counteract this, be more positive and go *ahead* on the *opposite* engine to the wind with *slightly* more throttle than normal.

Likewise when entering a berth with a strong crosswind the bow can be blown off as the boat slows down, so you can't complete the turn.

It's better to go past the berth and turn right around so you can use the wind to help blow the bow into the berth and tighten the turn.

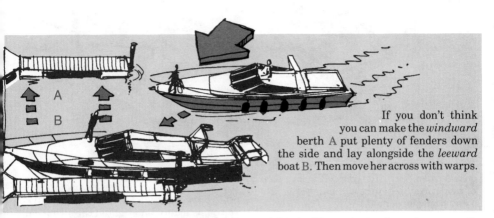

If you don't think you can make the *windward* berth A put plenty of fenders down the side and lay alongside the *leeward* boat B. Then move her across with warps.

It often helps to land a crew person at an easier position in the marina and get them to walk around to take your lines at the awkward berth.

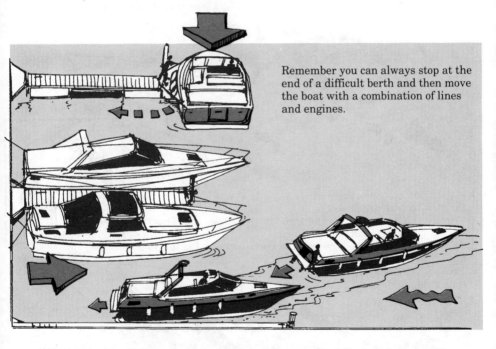

Remember you can always stop at the end of a difficult berth and then move the boat with a combination of lines and engines.

Sometimes it's easier to back into position (especially with stern drives) as the bow will *weathercock* downwind and simply follow the stern in (a bit like a front-wheel drive car). And if there's a strong tide, as above, opposing the wind the braking effect of putting the engines in *ahead* is greater than using *reverse*.

BUT REMEMBER ALWAYS USE THE **LEAST** POSSIBLE POWER FOR THE PREVAILING CONDITIONS.

LEAVING ALONGSIDE

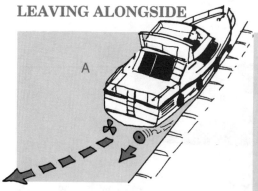

Protect the curve of the bow with fenders and go *astern* on the *inside* prop. If you've plenty of room the *offset* effect will pull her gently away from the dock (A)

If you're learning or there's an onshore wind, or if you're in a tight spot, a bow line will stop you going astern and tighten the swing out (B). Rig it from the *outside* fairlead to help her turn and give her a touch *ahead* on the *outside* prop to settle the bow on the fender.

With practice, even in onshore winds, you'll be able to leave the dock without any lines.
1. Go *astern* on the *inside* prop and *ahead* on the *outside* one. This will bring the stern out.
2. Having the helm turned towards the dock increases the turning force.
3. Balance the props until clear then straighten her up.

STERNDRIVE
Here is a case for *NOT* using opposite helm and engine. Turn helm to the *left* and put the *left* engine in *reverse*. This tends to *lift* the boat from the dock.

MOORING BUOYS

There are several types of mooring buoy so motor gently past to see how you'll need to attach yourself to it.

When ready motor into the current and stop so the crew can make fast.

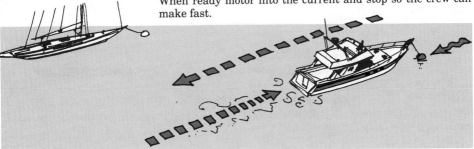

(A) With a high bow it's sometimes better to motor past keeping the *stern into the wind* and attach a bowline led back to the stern. Use the engine *away* from any stray lines on the buoy to hold her position.

A

(B) A lassoo (see page 21) dropped right over the buoy will hold you while you secure a bow line.

MOORING TO PILES

1. Prepare lines and a fender fore and aft.
2. Nudge the bow just past the post, so the crew can make fast the bow line.
3. Back off with *outside* prop so she starts to swing, see page 38.
4. Adjust the bowline so the quarter, NOT the vulnerable stern, touches the post.
5. Attach stern line and centre up between piles.

ANCHORING

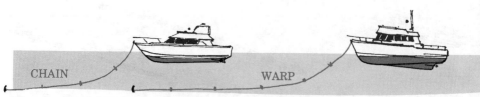

CHAIN   WARP

All anchors work best if the pull on them is close to horizontal. To achieve this the anchor cable must be given plenty of 'SCOPE'.

A nylon rope absorbs shock but needs at least 5m of chain near the anchor to resist chafe. A simple 'rule of thumb' for scope is chain (4 x depth) warp (6 x depth). If bad weather is expected (10 x depth) may be needed.

FINDING THE RIGHT SPOT
This is not easy in a crowded anchorage - try to judge your neighbours' swinging circles and have a guess who might drag in the middle of the night! (A) Cruise around and get a *'picture'* of the bottom with you echo-sounder and don't choose a spot (B) where if the anchor does drag it will drop off the edge.

LOWERING THE ANCHOR

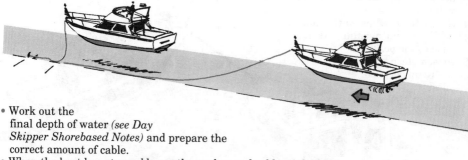

- Work out the final depth of water *(see Day Skipper Shorebased Notes)* and prepare the correct amount of cable.
- When the boat has *stopped* lower the anchor and cable as the boat reverses back.
- Always allow for the anchor dragging slightly before it bites.
- Make sure the cable is paid out evenly so it doesn't lay in a heap on the anchor.
- When the right *'scope'* is out, make fast and *'set'* the anchor by applying a *little* extra reverse.

IS IT HOLDING?

• Line up some shore-marks to see if you are dragging.

• If you are lying beam-on to the wind at slack water you are dragging.
• Feel the cable and if it's vibrating unduly - you're dragging.
• If in any way you feel unsure don't just put out more chain - get the anchor up and re-lay it.

TRIPPING LINES

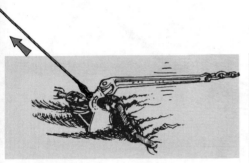

If you think your anchor might get stuck - add a tripping line to the other end of the anchor so you can pull it free.

These lines can foul the propellers and keels etc., so add a weight to sink it down out of harm's way.

WEIGHING ANCHOR

1. A touch of 'ahead' will take the load off the cable while the crew or capstan hauls it in.
2. If the anchor is stuck 'take a turn' when the cable is straight up and down and let the momentum of the boat 'break it out'.

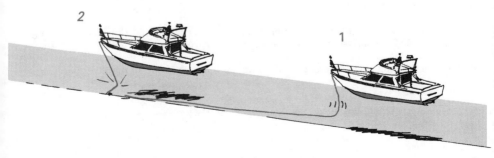

GOOD MANNERS
SOME DO'S AND DONT'S

DO - Avoid *speeding near moored boats* where people might be *sleeping, unloading gear from dinghies, working aloft or children might be sailing.* It only takes a few seconds to drive a boat well clear and creates a good seamanlike impression.

DO - Avoid large fleets of sailing boats and be aware that they have to *tack* or zig-zag into the wind.

WHEN ALONGSIDE

DO - Tidy up the boat and all the lines

DO - Use some time to clean the boat.

DO - Take down the ensign at night when moored. It's a custom that the ensign isn't flown in harbour from sunset or 2100 to 0800. In winter from sunset to 0900.

DO - Secure the dinghy so it won't get in the way or bump the boat all night.

DON'T - Cross other people's boats by going through their cockpits. Respect their privacy and go around by the foredeck.

DON'T - Look into hatches or ports (windows).

DON'T - Jump onto decks.

DON'T - Stand on stanchions, guardrails, hatches or varnishwork.

DON'T - Cross people's decks singing and shouting. (Remember you'll be the inside boat one day - so set a good example by walking quietly.)

DON'T - Sit in the cockpit or flybridge talking loudly into the small hours - your neighbours might be trying to sleep - go below.

DON'T - Eat and drink too much if you are cruising the next day.

DON'T - Throw rubbish into the water.

POWER TRIM

Power trim swings the outdrive leg in or out. This alters the angle of the propeller's thrust.

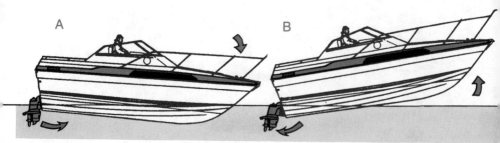

(A) Pull the leg in and the bow will come down. (B) Push the leg out and the bow will rise.

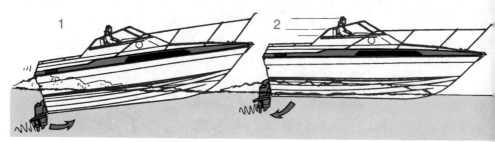

1. Have the leg right in to start. This will help the boat get up on to the plane.

2. When on the plane gradually ease the leg out to achieve the highest speed.

3. If the boat starts to porpoise (bow starts going up and down) readjust the leg.

4. When the leg is set correctly for the conditions the boat will ride level.

The trim of the boat can affect *fuel consumption, comfort,* and *safety in heavy weather,* see page 50.

Like all trim controls the gauges in the wheelhouse only show an approximate leg angle, so you'll need to experiment to find the optimum angle for any given sea state. Likewise the controls should only be pressed for 2 seconds and then WAIT to see what happens. Many seem to be wired up in a confusing manner, so check that the commands from the wheelhouse and the flybridge match.

Trim can be affected by the number of people on board and the amount of fuel in the tanks - as you burn more, usually the stern will rise. So you'll need to re-trim.

TRIM TABS

Trim tabs are metal flaps that can be raised or lowered together or independently, to alter the attitude of the boat both fore and aft and athwartships (sideways). The controls can be confusing. Both these on the right are doing the same thing! (*lowering the port bow.*)

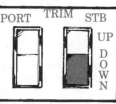

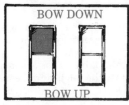

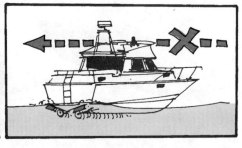

In breezy conditions, lightweight boats with a lot of windage might find slow manoeuvres easier with the tabs down *gripping* the water.

Try not to forget about the tabs as reversing with them down could cause damage to the less robust models.

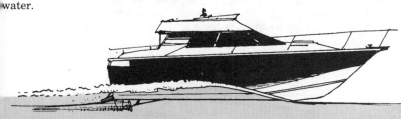

Ideally boats should get up onto the plane without using the tabs but many benefit from having the tabs fully down, to help lift a heavy stern. They only start working efficiently at speeds over 15 knots and then they can have a considerable effect on fuel consumption. Experiment to find the optimum angle for fuel economy and speed.

Although in practice the optimum angle is often a compromise between max speed, best fuel consumption, minimum slamming and maximum spray deflection, usually it works at approximately 3/4 7/8 maximum deflection but each boat is different, so experiment.

49

HEAVY WEATHER

Beam or
quartering wind

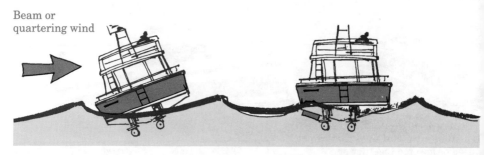

Usually trim tabs are operated together, but in these conditions the bow gets pushed and the helmsman subconsciously counteracts by steering into the wind. This tends to make the boat lean *into* the wind. Lower the windward tab to keep her level. Care must be taken as *one tab down* can steer her slightly off course. Tabs are more effective than power trim as they are further apart but do remember the tab is down, especially if you turn right around.

HEAD SEA TRIM

With the tabs up the bow will rise and the seas will *slam* into the bottom of the boat. Gradually ease them down so the sharper part of the bow *pierces* the waves. This will also improve vision over the bow as well as the spray deflection. Some outdrive boats might need the leg pulling in to push the bow down and to get the prop deeper in the water.

FOLLOWING SEA TRIM

If the tabs are *down* the bow will be *down* and a following sea might pick up the stern and the bow will get deeper and 'trip' the boat sideways (broach, see opposite page). To avoid this have the tabs *up* so the bows are *up*. Adjust your speed to be either *faster* or *slower* than the following seas, as it takes a very experienced helmsman to keep the boat riding on the back of a wave. (They might also set the tabs differently).

Don't smash straight into large waves as it will cause unnecessary strain on both the boat and crew. Zig-zag up them so the gradient is less (like hill climbing) and try to avoid any breaking crests.

BROACHING

This is when a large, quartering or following sea picks up the stern and tries to push the boat sideways. In bad cases the boat could be rolled on to its side. With quartering waves try keeping the leeward trim tab down to keep her upright.

If it starts to happen - unfortunately the two engines make it worse. The *port* prop is lifted into 'frothy' water, while the *starboard* one is driven deeper into solid water, turning her even more! You must turn hard to starboard and if necessary slow the starboard engine. As she comes back on course straighten the helm and synchronise engine revs. If it keeps happening - SLOW DOWN!

DAMAGE CONTROL

If a window gets smashed turn that part of the boat away from the seas and try to block the hole with wood or the cabin carpet etc. Then run slowly *downwind* and keep the coastguard informed of your progress.

MAN OVERBOARD

There is no *ideal* man overboard drill but this system works both day and night.

1. Shout 'man overboard' and note the course.
2. Put the helm over so you *add about 50°* to your course. (Here we're going due North 000°(M) so we turn until the compass reads 050°(M).) This angle varies from boat to boat so experiment.
3. When the course reads course + 50° put the *helm hard over* the other way.
4. When you're on a *reciprocal course* (180°to original course) cut the throttles.
   The casualty should be somewhere in a small area ahead of you.

THE APPROACH

5. Motor slowly towards him aiming about 10ft off to windward, on the helmsman's side. This means the helmsman will always be able to see him and the boat won't be blowing away from him.
6. Prepare a line and stop the near side prop. If you're liable to drift over him, go ahead on the offside engine and bring your stern into the wind. Many boats are easier to control in this position with strong winds and any large waves will make you both go up and down and not crash you into one another. Control your position by going ahead or astern on the engine away from the casualty if possible.
7. If you're not sure of your boat handling skills make contact with a long floating line.

BUT DON'T GET IT ROUND THE PROP!

RECIPROCAL COURSE

180

4

3

HE MUST BE AHEAD OF US

HELM HARD OVER

APPROX. **50°**

50

2

0

1

Rig a long ladder, lower the dinghy or use some form of *crane* to get the casualty on board. Wet people are **very heavy**, so practise using the davits or anchor windlass as lifting devices.

PRACTISE WITH YOUR CREW AS **YOU** MIGHT BE THE ONE IN THE WATER!

TOWING

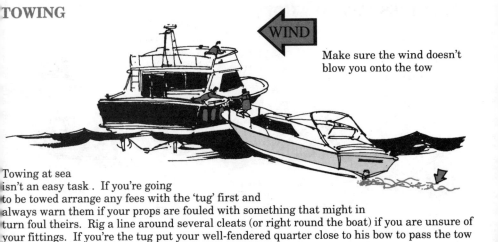

Make sure the wind doesn't blow you onto the tow

Towing at sea isn't an easy task . If you're going to be towed arrange any fees with the 'tug' first and always warn them if your props are fouled with something that might in turn foul theirs. Rig a line around several cleats (or right round the boat) if you are unsure of your fittings. If you're the tug put your well-fendered quarter close to his bow to pass the tow line.

The tow line needs to be protected from chafe and long enough to stop it 'snatching' in heavy seas (50 metres is not too long in big waves). Shorten the tow in smooth waters. Some people use the casualty's anchor chain, as this is strong, resists chafe and is heavy - so its weight acts as a shock-absorber when it hangs in a long curve. In fact any weight on the line (such as an anchor) helps to stop 'snatching'. A bridle to both quarters is probably best if you don't have a central fairlead. This will spread the load and stop the 'tow' pulling you off course.

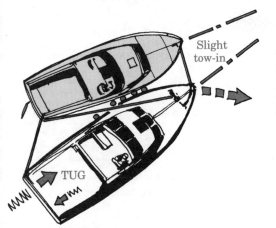

Slight tow-in

TUG

TOWING ALONGSIDE
Inside the harbour rig the boats like this with large fenders between them. Remember you might have to use the casualty's rudder or a touch *astern* on the inside engine to turn the two craft, only in smooth waters and mind your fingers!

WHO GIVES WAY TO WHO?

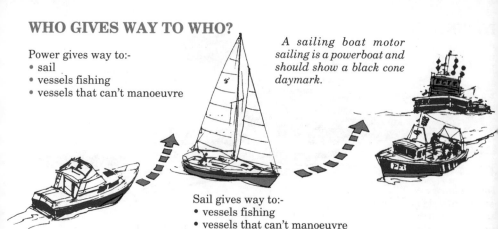

Power gives way to:-
• sail
• vessels fishing
• vessels that can't manoeuvre

A sailing boat motor sailing is a powerboat and should show a black cone daymark.

Sail gives way to:-
• vessels fishing
• vessels that can't manoeuvre

RULES OF THE ROAD

Head-on both turn to starboard.

(A) has to give way to any vessel in this sector.

Any vessel, power or sail, has to give way when overtaking in this sector.

SHIPS You must keep a good look-out.

Small vessels must give way to large vessel in what is to them *a narrow channel*.

Ships can appear from over the horizon and be on top of you in 10 mins!

FOG

In fog a power vessel *of any size* (when underway) will give a *long blast every 2 mins*. A sailing boat sounds *one long and two short*.

LIGHTS

A powerboat must show these lights when underway at night. The masthead light must be at least one metre above the sidelights and the colours and cut-off angles give a clue to the direction of travel.

GREEN WHITE
WHITE
RED

WHAT YOU SEE IN DAYLIGHT

WHAT YOU SEE AT NIGHT

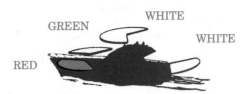

T ANCHOR   **MOTORSAILING**

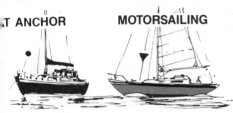

he relationship between a ship's 2 white masthead ghts shows in which direction it is travelling.

The front masthead white light is the lower

FISHING   FISHING GEAR OUT 150m IN THIS DIRECTION

TRAWLING

PILOT VESSEL   **HOVERCRAFT**

ALL ROUND FLASHING YELLOW LIGHT

TOWING   **VESSEL CANNOT MANOEUVRE**

over 200m

RESTRICTED IN ABILITY TO MANOEUVRE BUT MAKING WAY.

MINE SWEEPING   **UNDER WATER WORK**

SAFE SIDE   DANGER SIDE

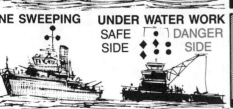

55

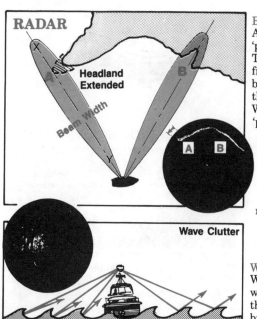

BEAM WIDTH

A radar beam sweeps through 360° and 'paints' a picture of the reflected signals. The beam width of a yacht's radar can be from 2° to 6° wide. So at *1 mile range* the beam could be about *200 metres across* and this gives problems:-

When the beam hits headland A, it starts to 'paint' but uses the aerial's centre-line X-Y as its reference. This extends the headland picture and makes a bearing on it unreliable.

At B, the beam width is so wide it ignores the inlet and 'paints' a continuous coastline. But here the range is more reliable as the object is at 90°to the beam.

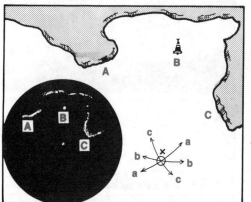

WAVE CLUTTER

Wave clutter is caused by the waves to windward reflecting the signals back better than those to leeward. This can be reduced by careful tuning, although heavy rain can still be a problem.

POSITION FIX BY RADAR RANGE

Radar can be used to plot a position by using either a visual bearing and a radar range or three radar ranges. Here we have two conspicuous headlands A and C and buoy B. By striking off their ranges we get a fix at X. *BUT, as a line of parked cars can give a stronger signal than a low coastline, so care is always needed when interpreting a radar picture!*

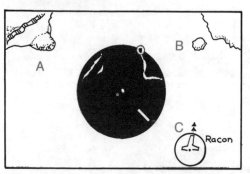

A radar screen needs careful tuning and an experienced eye to interpret it.

It *does not* show a 'bird's eye view'. A low lying headland backed by cliffs (A) will look like and island while a small island could look like a headland (B).

Racons (C) are electronic devices that mark the screen with a line radiating away from their position.

RADAR PLOT
Collision avoidance.

If an approaching vessel maintains the same bearing to us, there will be a collision. A radar can check the approach just like a hand bearing compass - and a simple plot will show which way he's heading.

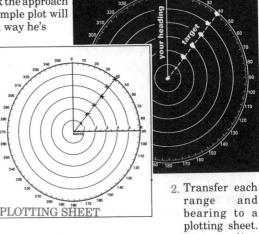

1. Hold a *steady* course. Plot vessel every 6 min. (6 min = 1/10 hr) makes sums easy, just move the decimal point.

PLOTTING SHEET

2. Transfer each range and bearing to a plotting sheet. Draw line through mean approach.

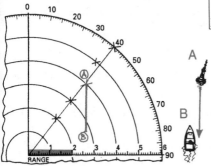

3. We're doing 20 knots - so every 6 mins we'll cover 2 miles. Choose any plot (A) and assume he was stationary in the water, like a buoy. In 6 mins his position (B) would have moved towards us 2 miles. (20 knots for 6 mins = 2 miles).

1.5 miles x 10 = 15 knots

4. *BUT* his position after 6 mins was (C). Join (B) (C) to give his approach angle. Measure (B) (C) to give his speed (15 knots).

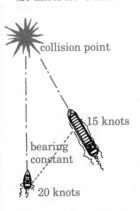

collision point

15 knots

bearing constant

20 knots

5. This is a seagull's eye view of the situation

What do we do?

6. Slow down to 4 knots and he'll pass quickly ahead of us. (If he's seen us on radar we'll have virtually stopped - showing we're a small boat and no threat).

7. If you're totally confused - **STOP**. Then, if you keep the heading steady - all tracks are **real** and not **relative**.

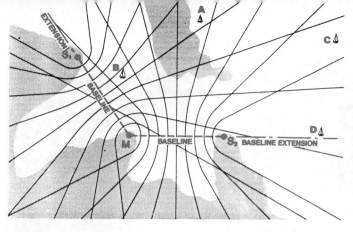

DECCA

Radio signals from a *master* and two *slave* transmitters create a hyperbolic position fixing grid. The receiver onboard senses the phase difference between the master and the slave signals and displays the position as either lat. and long. coordinates or DECCA grid reference numbers.

The accuracy can be affected by:

- Grid pattern distorted by propagation differences between land and sea. (Radio waves bend slightly when crossing between land and sea: this is a fixed error A.)

- Range from the transmitters (max. 240 miles by day, less by night.)

- Position in the grid - B will be more accurate than C due to the relative sizes of the grid 'diamonds'.

- Being too close to the *base line extension* (position D). The cure is to switch to a different 'chain' of transmitters.

- Electrical interference onboard from powerful radios etc.

- Thunderstorms near the boat or worse still near the transmitter where you are unaware of them.

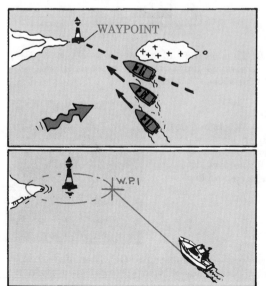

WAYPOINTS

A lat. or long. WAYPOINT position can be programmed into the set and the range of bearing to that point constantly read out. Some sets can also cope with tidal vectors, variation, deviation, speed and course over the ground as well as being interfaced with other electronic instruments.

It is very important to keep up a plot on the chart and to make an allowance for the tide. If you don't, the instrument will keep giving out an up-dated RANGE and BEARING *but* you could be swept into a danger area without realizing it. Some machines will show the *CROSS-TRACK ERROR*.

Many people sight the waypoint 1/2 mile to the *safe side* of a prominent point to avoid a 'DECCA induced collision', if the readings are slightly out.

GPS

Unlike DECCA which can only be used in specific areas, GPS (*Global Positioning System*) will give you your position anywhere in the world. The satellites used have a random error built in for civilian use but most sets will display *the degree of uncertainty* of the position. To maintain high accuracy the correct datum for the chart you are using must also be set into the machine otherwise you could be over 100 metres out. Like all new electronic equipment it is improving all the time and can be interfaced with other electronic instruments such as auto-pilots and chart plotters.

BUT LIKE ANYTHING ELSE THEY CAN GO WRONG!
So always keep a separate record of your progress in the logbook and on your chart.

ECHO-SOUNDERS

This relatively simple electronic instrument measures the time difference between a transmitted and reflected signal and converts it into a depth reading.

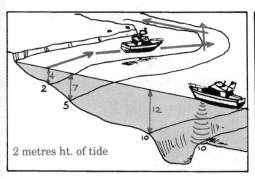

2 metres ht. of tide

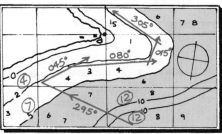

Here the chart has been marked with the echo-sounder readings we would expect with 2 metres height of tide and the bearings to follow the relative contours.

Pre-set depth alarms are useful features on an echo-sounder and are not just used to show shallows or distinctive sea-bed features. By setting them (allowing for height of tide and depth of transducer) a quite accurate course can be made in restricted visibility by following a depth contour line. Work out a course or courses to correspond to the contour line then follow along it using the alarms or by watching the depth readings.

PASSAGE MAKING
FROM RED RIVER TO GREEN BAY - APPROX 50M

Boat Speed: 20 knots.
Wind: Northerly Force 4.

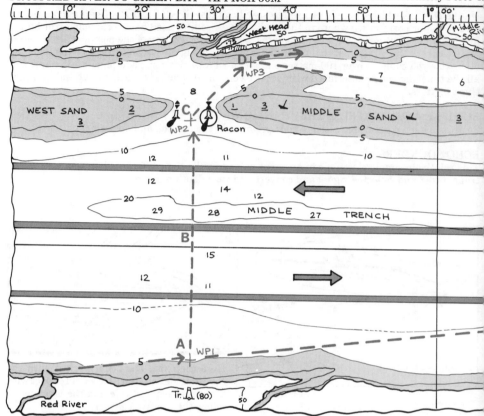

A. Fix position at departure point. Alter course to 000°(T). Don't forget compass deviation and variation. Be aware of ships approaching on port side in separation scheme. Enter time and distance run into logbook. Plot Decca fix every 15 minutes.

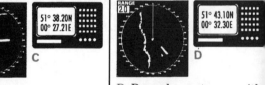

B. With radar identify Racon on West cardinal buoy. Echo sounder confirms Decca position. Be aware of ships approaching on starboard side.

C. Buoys now visible abeam. Alter course to 045 ° (T). Identify West Head on radar and visually. Decca agrees with radar and visual position.

D. Decca does not agree with radar and echo sounder - ignore Decca! Alter course to 097 ° (T). Make sure radar range from Middle Cliff does not exceed 3 miles to keep clear of Middle Sand (which is just under water). Watch echo sounder. East cardinal buoy will be visible from about 2 miles.

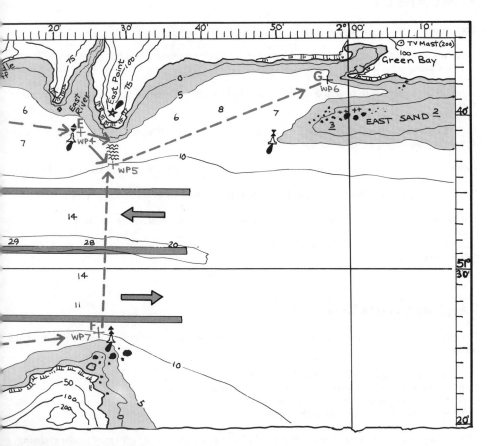

E. Decca now agrees with radar and visual fix. If conditions are moderate go inside tidal race off East Point, 100 °(T). Radar range no less than 1 mile off. If rough, go outside race. At Waypoint 5. Alter course to 070° (T).

51° 38.81N
01° 23.55E

E

F. If the wind was southerly, A to F would have been a better route. Identify North cardinal at F and alter course to cross the shipping lanes at right angles. Use radar to identify East Point and ensure a safe distance off.

51° 25.95N
01° 28.83E

F

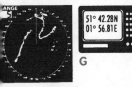

G. Radar position and Decca position confirmed visually. Slow down, check you know where you are before deciding course to steer. Stop if unsure. Prepare for berthing or mooring.

51° 42.28N
01° 56.81E

G

REMEMBER :

Provision adequately and ensure that everything is stowed securely.

Have an alternative strategy for bad weather or any unforseen problems. Be flexible in your passage plan.

Most lifeboat rescues to disabled motor cruisers could easily be avoided by simple maintenance checks.

At 20 knots you will be covering one mile every three minutes. Prepare your navigation plan in advance. You might easily miss the change of depth at B.

Don't sit glued to the Decca or radar screen. Use one to confirm the other and keep a good lookout.

You can always slow down if you need time to think or to interpret the radar picture.

Before manoeuvring brief the crew - it saves shouting from the steering position.

Don't give orders such as "OK on the bow". Give instructions - "Let go forward", "Hold on aft", "Make fast aft".

TAKING COMMAND.

The success of your motor cruising depends entirely on you, the skipper. Your crew will come back for more if you :

Can navigate - attend an RYA shorebased course.
Can handle the boat - attend an RYA practical course.
Give calm instructions - shouting is rarely necessary.
Take responsibility - don't blame the crew.

The more you know the more relaxed you will be and the more you will enjoy motor cruising.

PILOTAGE

Pilotage is the skill of navigating in confined waters. There will seldom be time to plot fixes and EPs so you need to use other means to keep track of your position and course to steer.

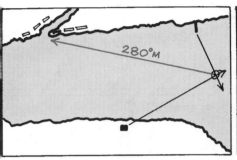

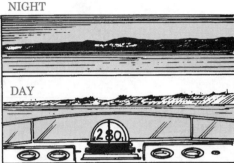

It's not always easy to identify a harbour entrance. So check its rough bearing from your charted position.

Then go on deck and turn the boat until the compass reads the same bearing. The harbour should be somewhere ahead.

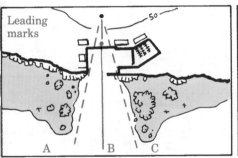

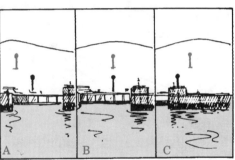

Some harbours guide you in with leading marks or lights - when they're in line you're on course.

A. We're off to port.
B. The marks are in line, we're on course.
C. We're off to starboard.

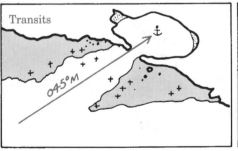

You can make your own *leading marks* or *transits*. From the chart we see if we head for the harbour edge on 045°(M) we'll miss the rocks.

Point at the edge of the harbour when on 045°(M) and see what lines up with it. If we keep the tree and 'edge' in line we'll miss the rocks.

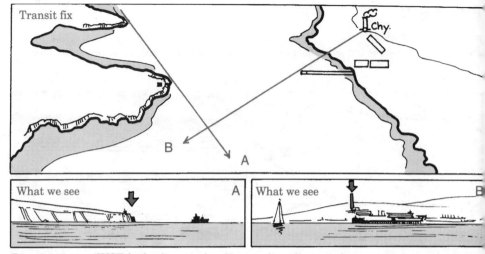

Transits are not JUST for leading marks. You can literally 'see where you are' on a chart by lining up two transits. Here the two headlands give one transit and the chimney and pier another.

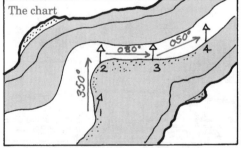

Here we have drawn a line 070°(M) to the buoy. Provided our compass always reads *more* than 070°(M) we shall be clear of the shallow water.

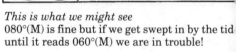

This is what we might see
080°(M) is fine but if we get swept in by the tid until it reads 060°(M) we are in trouble!

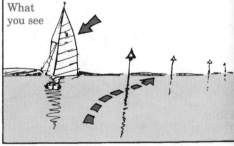

Channel markers look very clear on the chart but when you get there they can be quite confusing. It helps to mark bearing lines on the chart so you know where to look for the next one.

Here it looks as if we can just follow the starboard marks in - but 'look at the chart', No 2 marks 'dog leg' but it's hidden by the boat in front! It' too easy to go from 1 to 3 thinking it's the nex mark.